W9-CNC-569

Cornerstones of Freedom

The Disability Rights Movement

Deborah Kent

CHILDREN'S PRESS®
A Division of Grolier Publishing
New York • London • Hong Kong • Sydney
Danbury, Connecticut

Library of Congress Cataloging-in-Publication Data

Kent, Deborah.
    The disability-rights movement / by Deborah Kent.
      p.   cm.—(Cornerstones of freedom)
Includes index.
    Summary: Traces the development of the disability-rights
movement in fighting discrimination against the handicapped
and in securing civil rights for the disabled.
    ISBN 0-516-06632-3
    1. Handicapped—Civil rights—United States—Juvenile literature.
2. Discrimination against the handicapped—United States—Juvenile
literature. 3. Sociology of disability—United States—Juvenile
literature. [1. Handicapped—Civil rights. 2. Discrimination.]
I. Title. II. Series.
HV1553.K45 1996
323.3-dc20

95-40359
CIP
AC

Six-year-old Judy Heumann couldn't wait to start school. From the window of her family's Brooklyn apartment, she watched other children hurrying along the sidewalk with their bookbags and lunchboxes, and longed to join them. But when her mother took her to register, the school principal said that she could not enroll.

Judy had developed polio when she was eighteen months old, and she used a wheelchair to move about. The principal insisted that the school was not designed for a student who couldn't walk, and that there was no way Judy could fit into the program for "normal" children. She was put on home instruction, a teacher visiting her apartment for an hour or two three times a week.

Judy Heumann had polio as a child and has used a wheelchair ever since.

Paul Steven Miller graduated near the top of his class at Harvard Law School. But when he began searching for a job, he was turned down by one law firm after another. Because of his short stature, or dwarfism, employers did not believe that Miller could be an effective attorney. At one job interview he was told that clients might "think we're running some kind of circus freak show."

Ruth Sienkiewicz developed cerebral palsy after an illness when she was an infant. She could not speak or move her arms and legs. She communicated with her family by raising her eyes to say yes and lowering her gaze to say no. When Ruth was twelve, her parents decided they could no longer care for her at home.

They placed her in Belchertown State Hospital, an institution run by the state of Massachusetts for people with mental retardation. She lay in a hospital ward, with no schooling, no outings, nothing to look forward to but a visit home once a year at Christmas. The hospital staff kept her alive, but treated her as though she were a subhuman creature without thoughts or feelings.

According to 1990 census figures, about 43 million Americans, or one person out of every seven, have some form of disability. A disability is defined as any condition that limits a person's capacity to work or to perform tasks of daily living such as dressing, bathing, cooking, driving an automobile, or using a telephone. People with disabilities form the largest minority group in the United States. African-Americans, the next largest minority, are estimated to number 30 million.

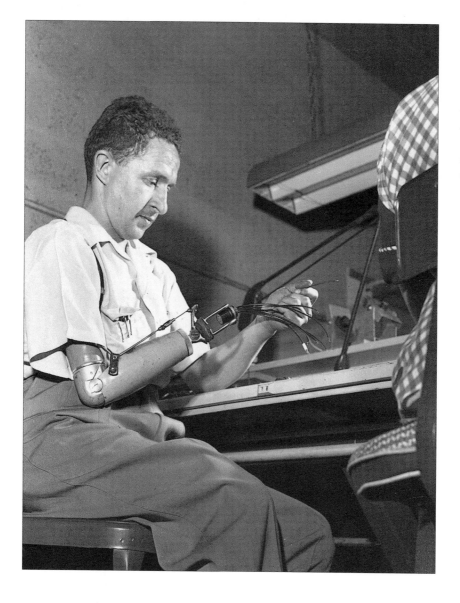

For many years, disabled people have struggled to obtain jobs. This is Lee Hyatt, who worked in an electronics plant in the 1950s. He did his job with a prosthetic arm.

A schoolteacher with a special needs student

The term "disability" embraces an extremely wide assortment of conditions. The disabled population includes people who use wheelchairs or crutches; people who are totally blind or have low vision; persons who are deaf or hard of hearing; people with mental retardation, cerebral palsy, or learning disabilities; people with such chronic diseases as diabetes, AIDS, arthritis, cancer, and asthma; and people with psychiatric illnesses such as schizophrenia and depression.

Judy Heumann, Paul Miller, and Ruth Sienkiewicz have widely varied disabling conditions. Yet they share one common bond. Each of them experienced the pain of discrimination. Like millions of other Americans, they were denied education, employment, and even the most basic human dignity, simply because of their disabilities.

Throughout history, people with disabilities have made lasting contributions to society. Homer, the greatest poet of ancient Greece, was blind. Ludwig van Beethoven was deaf when he composed his magnificent Ninth Symphony. President Franklin D. Roosevelt had had polio and used a wheelchair.

But these disabled "super-stars" were the fortunate exceptions. For the most part, people who were blind, deaf, or unable to walk were long treated as outcasts or as pitiable objects of charity. Rarely were they expected or permitted to study, to work, to raise families, or to play any meaningful part in the life of the community.

President Franklin D. Roosevelt lost the use of his legs when he contracted polio.

In 1940, a group of blind men and women from seven states gathered in Wilkes-Barre, Pennsylvania. The group founded an organization called the National Federation of the Blind, "to promote the economic and social welfare of the blind." It was the first time that people with a specific disability organized on a national level to fight for their rights. The federation's first president, Jacobus tenBroek, was a California lawyer. At that time, he was one of the few blind people who had ever achieved

Geraldine Lawhorn, (left), who was blind and deaf, was a teacher in Chicago for more than forty years.

such success. In a speech at the Wilkes-Barre convention, tenBroek declared, "It is necessary for the blind to organize themselves and their ideas upon a national basis, so that blind [people] the nation over can live in physical comfort, social dignity, and spiritual self-respect." Decades later, the National Federation of the Blind served as the model for other organizations of people with disabilities as they struggled for full participation in society.

With a small amount of assistance, this blind person can participate in society.

When Ed Roberts contracted polio at the age of fourteen, one doctor told his parents that it would be better for him to die than to survive as a cripple. When he recovered from his illness, Roberts was a quadriplegic—he had lost the use of his arms and legs. Like Judy Heumann, he was refused admission by his local school. His parents battled the school board until he was finally able to attend high school. He ran into similar roadblocks when he applied to college.

Wheelchair ramps make buildings accessible to disabled people.

In 1962, he persuaded the University of California at Berkeley to give him a chance. But Roberts found that he could get into only a few of the classroom buildings. Most of the buildings on campus had steps for people who could walk, but no ramps or elevators that could be used by someone in a wheelchair.

Despite these problems, Roberts excelled at Berkeley. His success encouraged the university to accept other disabled students. By 1967, twelve wheelchair users were attending classes. They all felt frustrated because stairs and narrow doorways made much of the campus inaccessible to them. They were also angered by their dealings with the rehabilitation system. Under state and federal law, the Department of

Rehabilitation was supposed to help disabled students pay for whatever special equipment or services they needed to reach their goals. But few rehabilitation counselors were disabled themselves. Most did not really believe that disabled people could lead productive lives. Instead of helping them, the rehab counselors seemed to thwart the Berkeley students at every turn.

In 1970 Ed Roberts won a government grant to start a special program for physically disabled students at Berkeley. Roberts's program was staffed entirely by people with disabilities. Drawing on their own experiences, they counseled the disabled students. They kept lists of wheelchair-accessible apartments, and pressured the university to install ramps and curb cuts.

Soon disabled people who were not students were asking for help as well. In 1972, Roberts obtained funding to expand the program, which was called the Center for Independent Living (CIL). Similar programs sprang up in other California cities and across the nation. The independent living movement, as it came to be known, helped people with disabilities take control over their own lives. Its leaders recognized that people with disabilities shared much with African-Americans and people of other racial minorities. "We were talking about self-empowerment, self-hatred, and discrimination," Roberts said later. "All the same issues."

In the spring of 1970, at the same time Ed Roberts was starting the first independent living program, Judy Heumann ran into a wall of prejudice in New York City. Like Roberts, she had finally been admitted to public school after a long, fierce battle. She attended Long Island University and planned to become a teacher. But New York City refused to issue her a teaching license. School officials claimed that she would not be able to control her students or help them in an emergency. Heumann sued the Board of Education for discrimination, and the press took up her cause. "We're not going to let a hypocritical society give us a token education and then bury us!" she told the New York *Daily News*.

The paper carried her story under the headline, "YOU CAN BE PRESIDENT, NOT TEACHER, WITH POLIO." Eventually Judy Heumann won her fight and was permitted to teach in New York. The publicity over her case brought in a flood of letters and phone calls from disabled people who shared similar experiences. Over and over again, she learned of eager young people denied an education. She talked with qualified applicants who had been turned away from jobs, and grown men and women who lived with their parents because they could not support themselves or find accessible housing. All these separate voices merged to form a great chorus, crying out for justice.

Judy Heumann believed that people with disabilities must work together to pass laws that would ensure their civil rights. In the fall of 1970, at the age of 22, she founded Disabled in Action (DIA), an organization dedicated to bringing about political change. In 1972 DIA and other disability groups demonstrated at the Lincoln Memorial in Washington, D.C., after President Richard Nixon vetoed a bill to fund programs for disabled people. Later that year Disabled in Action joined forces with a group of disabled veterans to occupy Nixon's New York campaign headquarters. The protesters demanded an on-camera debate with the president about disability issues. Though their demands were never met, their actions won wide press coverage.

Judy Heumann (right) and Ed Roberts (left) take part in a federal study of disability rights in 1982.

Few Americans had ever thought of the disabled as a minority group deprived of their rights. Fewer still expected to see people who used wheelchairs or crutches staging a political protest. Disabled people were supposed to be helpless and passive, to accept assistance with grateful smiles. But Disabled in Action had swept into the spotlight, demanding to be heard.

Disability rights activists such as Ed Roberts and Judy Heumann drew much of their inspiration from the movement for African-American civil rights that transformed America in the 1960s. When they heard black leaders speak of freedom and equality, they dared to

Some disability rights activists see their cause as similar to that of the civil rights movement; a key moment in African-Americans' struggle for rights was the march on Washington led by Martin Luther King in 1963 (right).

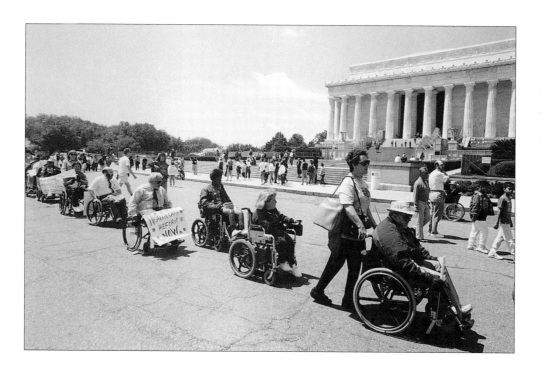

imagine a world without barriers for people with
disabilities. The leaders of the disability rights
movement recognized that a disabling condition,
such as blindness or cerebral palsy, need not
prevent anyone from living a full and rewarding
life. The real problem, they saw, was not the
disability itself. People with disabilities were
held back by the barriers that society put in
their way. There were "architectural barriers"
such as stairs and steep curbs, which kept many
disabled people from going to school, shopping,
or finding jobs. And there were wide-spread
"attitudinal barriers," the belief that people with
disabilities were useless, pathetic, and somehow
inferior. As long as such attitudes prevailed,
people with disabilities would never be valued
members of the community.

In 1973, a few lines at the end of a lengthy act of Congress gave the budding disability rights movement a great thrust forward. The crucial lines appeared at the end of Public Law 93–112, which reauthorized rehabilitation services for disabled people. Section 504 of the Rehabilitation Act of 1973 stated, "No otherwise qualified handicapped individual...shall, solely by reason of his handicap, be excluded from participation in...any program or activity receiving federal financial assistance."

No one knows for certain how these powerful words were written. Section 504 seemed tacked onto the Rehabilitation Act as little more than an afterthought. It was signed into law with no public comment or debate. But disability rights leaders realized at once that they had been handed a powerful tool. Schools, parks, libraries, post offices, hospitals, youth centers, city buses—all received funds from the federal government. Under Section 504, people with disabilities could no longer be barred from any of these facilities by architecture or attitudes.

While disabled activists celebrated, politicians and business leaders flung up their hands in dismay. Who would pay for ramps at the post office and elevators in the public library? How could the bus companies afford lifts for people who used wheelchairs? It was easy to make a

School buses equipped with wheelchair lifts help many disabled children get to and from school every day.

promise on paper, they argued, but where was the money going to come from?

Over the next four years, officials wrangled about how Section 504 should be carried out. By April 1977, the regulations for the new law lay on the desk of Joseph Califano, secretary of Health, Education, and Welfare (HEW), under President Jimmy Carter. The final regulations needed Califano's signature before the dream could become law. But Califano found one reason after another to stall. If too much time slipped by, Section 504 would never be implemented at all.

On April 5, people with disabilities demonstrated at the HEW headquarters in Washington, D.C., and at regional offices across the country. Led by Frank Bowe, who is deaf, some 300 disabled people took over Califano's Washington office for more than twenty-four hours. The most spectacular demonstration occurred in San Francisco under the direction of Judy Heumann. For twenty-five days, disabled people occupied San Francisco's HEW office. When officials shut down the telephone lines, deaf demonstrators stood at the windows and passed messages in American Sign Language to friends on the street below. When HEW tried to cut off the food supply to the building, sympathizers as diverse as McDonald's and the Black Panthers brought in provisions. "We all felt beautiful," recalled Mary Jane Owen, who is blind. "We all felt powerful. It didn't matter if you were mentally retarded, blind, or deaf. Everyone who came out felt 'We are beautiful, we are powerful, we are strong, we are important.'"

Pressured by the demonstrators and the publicity they stirred, Joseph Califano signed the regulations for Section 504 on April 28, 1977. The triumphant protesters left the HEW office, singing a song from the movement for black people's civil rights, "We Shall Overcome!"

In 1954, the U.S. Supreme Court ruled that "separate" was not "equal" in the education of African-American children. More than twenty years later, the federal government recognized the same principle in the education of children with disabilities. The Education for All Handicapped Children Act of 1975 (Public Law 94–142) stated that disabled children must be taught in "the least restrictive environment possible." No longer would children like Judy Heumann sit alone waiting for a home teacher to arrive, while their brothers and sisters hurried off to school. For the first time, federal law ensured that they could study and learn in public-school classrooms with their nondisabled peers.

By ramping sidewalk curbs, people in wheelchairs can move freely through neighborhoods and city streets.

A student in a wheelchair alongside his non-disabled classmates

Once these new laws were in place, people with disabilities still had battles to fight. By the 1990s, many children were still relegated to special "resource rooms" for disabled students, rather than being integrated into regular classrooms. Sixty-six percent of all disabled people of working age were still unemployed, though two-thirds of them claimed they could work and wanted to work. The public was slow to abandon its notion that disabled people were helpless and useless. Many people continued to think of life with a disability as a life not worth living.

In their struggle for equality, people with disabilities met ongoing resistance. Monetary cost was the most commonly cited argument against making buildings and programs fully accessible. Some measures, such as installing elevators, were indeed expensive. But costly changes were not usually necessary. A wheelchair lift, a simple device using a pulley, could be installed much more cheaply than an elevator. Sometimes all that was needed

A woman uses the first Braille automatic teller ever installed in New York City in 1986.

was a bit of creativity and common sense. A desk could be raised on blocks for a wheelchair to roll underneath; Braille labels could identify the buttons on an elevator. Every day, at home, at school, and on the job, disabled people quietly made suggestions and solved problems.

Some changes, however, came only after a major upheaval. The "Gallaudet Uprising" sent the issue of disability rights blazing across national headlines. Established in Washington, D.C., in 1864 as a college for the deaf, Gallaudet University had never been headed by a deaf president during its 124-year history. In March 1988, the president's chair was vacant again. Once more the board of trustees selected a hearing candidate to fill it. When students protested, they were told that deaf people were not ready to function in the hearing world. Outraged, students and faculty members staged a massive protest that shut down the university for a week. At last the trustees

A group of students block the entrance to Gallaudet University during the 1988 protest.

Dr. I. King Jordan, who was appointed as the first deaf president of Gallaudet University in 1988

appointed I. King Jordan, a deaf man who had previously served as dean of students. "This is a historic moment for deaf people around the world," Jordan said in his acceptance speech. "The world has watched the deaf community come of age. We can no longer accept limits on what we can achieve."

Dr. Jordan celebrates victory in the Gallaudet Uprising.

In the Gallaudet protests the public saw a group of disabled people fighting for respect and dignity, and emerging victorious. The stage was set for the most far-reaching piece of civil-rights legislation since the Voting Rights Act of 1965—the Americans with Disabilities Act (ADA). The stated purpose of the ADA was "to provide a clear and comprehensive national mandate for the elimination of discrimination against individuals with disabilities."

The law covered education, employment, transportation, telecommunications, public services, housing, and businesses. It envisioned a society in which all persons, disabled and nondisabled, would work and play together, would travel freely, and would have the opportunity to reach their fullest potential.

President George Bush signs the Americans with Disabilities Act in 1990. He is given a pen to sign the bill by Rev. Harold Wilke, a disability rights leader who has no arms.

On July 26, 1990, President George Bush signed the Americans with Disabilities Act into law. Three thousand people, many of them veterans of the disability-rights movement since its beginning twenty years before, gathered on the lawn of the White House to mark the occasion. It was a time for remembering and hope, for the joyful tears and laughter of celebration. "Let the shameful wall of exclusion finally come tumbling down!" President Bush declared, and everyone cheered those words of promise. At long last the law of the land ensured the full civil rights of people with disabilities.

Today, many city streets have curb cuts for people who use wheelchairs or crutches. Some buses are equipped with wheelchair lifts. Elevator panels in many public buildings are labeled in Braille. By dialing relay stations that use special teletypewriters, deaf people can now make telephone calls to friends, doctors, schools, and even pizza parlors. All of these changes have come about as a result of the ADA and other disability rights legislation. These improvements have also been made through the ongoing efforts of disabled people and their supporters.

The laws have not solved all of the problems faced by people with disabilities. Millions of disabled persons live in nursing homes and other institutions. They must live there because little funding is available for programs that would permit them to live in their own homes. Many public buildings and transit systems remain completely inaccessible to people who use wheelchairs. Another factor working against disabled people is unemployment. The unemployment rate among people with disabilities has risen in recent years. In 1986, 66 percent of disabled people of working age were unemployed. By 1994, unemployment within this group had reached 69 percent.

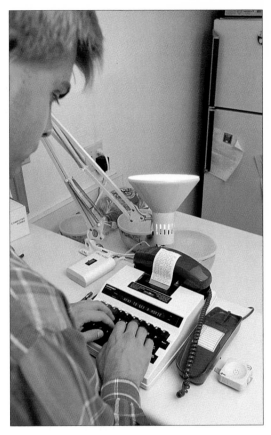

There are many ways in which simple changes can assist people with disabilities in daily life. Top left: A botanic garden installed signs with Braille to help blind people identify plants. Bottom: Parking lots have reserved spaces for disabled drivers. Top right: A hearing-impaired person uses a teletype phone to communicate with friends and relatives.

Many sports competitions, such as marathons, now include people with disabilities. Here, wheelchair racers begin a marathon in Chicago.

Though many challenges lie ahead, people with disabilities are becoming more visible on the streets, in the workplace, and in the media. As the public sees disabled athletes and actors, store clerks and teachers, the old image of disabled people as helpless is slowly worn away. In their work, their artistic achievements, and in the way they live from day to day, people with disabilities strive to show the world that their lives can be full and meaningful.

In the mid 1980s Cheryl Marie Wade, an actress who uses a wheelchair, founded "Wry Crips," a theater troupe of disabled women. Wry Crips stunned audiences with bold, irreverent, and often hilarious stories about their personal lives. To Wade, these performers were creating "disability art."

"Disability art," she reflects, "[means] identity. It expresses our connections to and our differences from people. Art defines us in our own words and our own images....Art embraces every complex part of who we are, alone and together, in this horrifying and exquisite journey."

Guides assist a blind woman on a ski slope.

GLOSSARY

activist Judy Heumann

activist – person who uses political means to champion a cause

cerebral palsy – any of several conditions caused by damage to the brain; it may involve uncontrolled movement, rigid muscles, and/or speech problems

depression – psychiatric condition in which a person feels sad and hopeless, regardless of actual circumstances

disability – any condition that limits a person's ability to work or perform tasks of daily living

discrimination – separate, unequal treatment based on some outward characteristic

dwarfism – any of several conditions that cause a person to have very short stature as an adult

integrate – to include in a group as an equal member

legislation – law

polio – a disease that can cause permanent damage to the body's muscles

prosthesis – an artificial limb

quadriplegia – the inability to use one's arms and legs

schizophrenia – a psychiatric illness in which a person loses touch with reality

prosthesis

TIMELINE

1864 Gallaudet University is established in Washington, D.C.

National Federation of the Blind **1940**
is established

Judy Heumann founds Disabled in Action **1970**

1972 ....
Ed Roberts
establishes the
Rehabilitation Act of 1973 approved **1973** first Center for
Independent
1975 Living

1988 Gallaudet University uprising

1990 George Bush signs the Americans with
Disabilities Act (ADA) into law

Education for All
Handicapped
Children Act is
passed

INDEX *(Boldface page numbers indicate illustrations.)*

African-Americans, 5, 11, 14, 19
Americans with Disabilities Act (ADA), 24, 25, 26
Beethoven, Ludwig van, 7
Belchertown State Hospital, 4
Black Panthers, 18
Bowe, Frank, 18
Bush, George, 25, **25**
Califano, Joseph, 17, 18
Carter, Jimmy, 17
Center for Independent Living (CIL), 11
Disabled in Action (DIA), 13, 14
Education for All Handicapped Children Act of 1975, 19

Gallaudet University, 22–24
Harvard Law School, 4
Heumann, Judy, 3, **3**, 6, 10, 12, **13**, 14, 18, 19
Homer, 7
Hyatt, Lee, **5**
Jordan, I. King, 23–24, **23, 24**
King, Martin Luther, **14**
Lawhorn, Geraldine, **8**
Lincoln Memorial, 13, **15**
McDonald's, 18
Miller, Paul Steven, 4, 6
National Federation for the Blind, 8–9
New York City, 12
New York *Daily News,* 12
Nixon, Richard, 13

Owen, Mary Jane, 18
Rehabilitation Act of 1973, 16
Roberts, Ed, 10–11, 12, **13,** 14
Roosevelt, Franklin Delano, 7, **7**
Sienkiewicz, Ruth, 4, 6
Supreme Court, U.S., 19
tenBroek, Jacobus, 8–9
Wade, Cheryl Marie, 29
Wilkes-Barre, Pennsylvania, 8
University of California (Berkeley), 10–11
Voting Rights Act of 1965, 24

PHOTO CREDITS

Cover, 1, AP/Wide World; 2, ©David Young-Wolff/Photo Edit; 3, Courtesy Assistant Secretary Special Education and Rehabilitative Services' Office; 5, UPI/Bettmann; 6, ©Paul Conklin/Photo Edit; 7, UPI/Bettmann; 8, AP/Wide World; 9, ©Stephen McBrady/Photo Edit; 10, ©Amy C. Etra/Photo Edit; 13, 14, 15, AP/Wide World; 17, ©Martin R. Jones/Unicorn Stock Photos; 19, ©David Young-Wolff/Photo Edit; 20, ©Jeff Greenberg/Unicorn Stock Photos; 21, 22, UPI/Bettmann; 23, AP/Wide World; 24, UPI/Bettmann; 25, Reuters/Bettmann; 27 (top left), ©Martha McBride/Unicorn Stock Photos; 27 (top right), ©Michael Newman/Photo Edit; 27 (bottom), ©Jean Higgins/Unicorn Stock Photos; 28, ©Joel Dexter/Unicorn Stock Photos; 29, ©James Fly/Unicorn Stock Photos; 30 (top), UPI/Bettmann; 30 (bottom), Courtesy Assistant Secretary Special Education and Rehabilitative Services' Office; 31 (top), AP/Wide World; 31 (middle), ©Jeff Greenberg/Unicorn Stock Photos; 31 (bottom), AP/Wide World

ADDITIONAL PICTURE IDENTIFICATIONS

Cover: Protesters demand access to the Empire State Building.

Page 1: Demonstrators attempt to block access to the Richard B. Russell Federal Building in Atlanta, Georgia, as part of a 1989 protest. The demonstrators were demanding that the building be made more accessible to disabled people.

STAFF

Project Editor: Mark Friedman
Design & Electronic Composition: TJS Design
Photo Editor: Jan Izzo
Cornerstones of Freedom Logo: David Cunningham

ABOUT THE AUTHOR

Deborah Kent grew up in Little Falls, New Jersey, where she was the first blind student to attend the local public school. She received her B.A. in English from Oberlin College and earned a master's degree from Smith College School for Social Work. For four years, she worked as a psychiatric social worker at the University Settlement House on New York's Lower East Side. She then spent five years in San Miguel de Allende, Mexico, where she wrote her first young-adult novel, *Belonging.* In San Miguel she helped to establish the town's first school for children with disabilities.

Deborah Kent lives in Chicago with her husband, children's writer R. Conrad Stein, and their daughter, Janna. She is the author of more than a dozen young-adult novels and numerous nonfiction books for children. She also writes articles on disability issues, and is an active member of the National Federation of the Blind.

DATE			